YRIE'S

PRACTICAL GUIDE
— TO —
COMMUNICATING

BIBLE

DOCTRINE

RYRIE'S

PRACTICAL GUIDE

TO

COMMUNICATING

BIBLE

DOCTRINE

CHARLES RYRIE

BROADMAN
& HOLMAN
PUBLISHERS

NASHVILLE, TENNESSEE

Ten-Digit ISBN: 0–8054–4063–1
Thirteen-Digit ISBN: 978–0–8054–4063–8

Published by Broadman & Holman Publishers
Nashville, Tennessee

Dewey Decimal Classification: 251
Subject Heading: PREACHING
DOCTRINAL THEOLOGY

Scripture quotations are from the New American Standard
Bible, © the Lockman Foundation, 1960, 1962, 1963, 1968,
1971, 1972, 1973, 1975, 1977, 1995; used by permission.

1 2 3 4 5 6 7 8 9 10 11 12 12 11 10 09 08 07 06 05

CONTENTS

Chapter One

---◆---

IS DOCTRINE REALLY THAT IMPORTANT?

When my grandsons, then ages ten and six, learned that their aunt was going to have a baby girl, their immediate response was a loud and disgusted "Yuck."

When the beautiful baby girl was born, their mother brought them to the hospital to see their new cousin. Both of them could hardly wait to hold the baby, and each took several turns at doing just that. Indeed, neither wanted to give her up.

Upon leaving the hospital on the way to the car, they both said to their mother, "We sure like that baby girl."

What happened to yuck?

Too many Christians have the yuck reaction to doctrine because they have never experienced the wonder and thrill of understanding, interacting, and embracing the doctrines (teachings) of God's wonderful Word.

Regrettably doctrine has fallen on hard times. Though true, this is not something new or unique to our day. Consider this lament from a prominent nineteenth-century churchman. He said, "Wherein do evangelical Churchmen fall short of their great predecessors in the eighteenth century? They fall short in doctrine. They are neither so full nor so distinct nor so uncompromising. They are afraid of strong statements. They are too ready to fence, and guard, and qualify all their teaching."[1]

More than a century later, a noted theologian evaluated (quite correctly in my judgment) the modern scene this way. "The new quest for contemporary practicality has transformed the nature of the Christian ministry, the work of seminaries, and the inner workings of denominational headquarters, and in each case the transformation has sounded the death knell of theology. . . . Resources have been steadily withdrawn from the publishing houses that have supported theological publication."[2] One has only to skim contemporary book catalogs to see how true that observation is. The proportion of doctrinal books in relation to plethora of other categories of books is small.

SOME EXCUSES (COP-OUTS!) FOR NEGLECTING DOCTRINE

Probably the most-often-heard objection to exposing people to doctrine is that it is not relevant. Experience is more important. Or to put it another way: doctrine is not practical. I have sat through hundreds of chapel periods in my lifetime. Hardly anything bothered me more than to hear a speaker say, "Now today I'm just going to be practical. I'll leave the teaching (doctrine) to your faculty." What a shallow statement. That speaker (and many others) forget that all practice must be based on sound Bible doctrine, and all Bible doctrine is expected to result in proper practice. Sound doctrine and biblical experiences have to be wedded. You must not have one without the other.

Relevant means "to have significant and demonstrable bearing on the matter at hand." *Practical* means "to relate to practice." Accusing doctrine of irrelevance or impracticality misuses both terms and assumes the Bible itself (from which our doctrine comes) is irrelevant and impractical. Of course, no one would want to make such a charge against the Word of God—at least not out loud.

Never forget what the Bible claims for itself. "All Scripture is inspired by God and profitable for teaching [very doctrinal], for reproof, for correction, for training in righteousness [very relevant]; so that the man of God may be adequate, equipped for every good work [very practical]" (2 Tim. 3:16–17). The word translated *adequate* means "proficient and able to meet all demands which are placed upon one's life." Putting the emphases of these two verses together, they clearly teach that biblical doctrine is not only relevant and practical but also provides the necessary proficiency for the believer's life and activities. There's nothing irrelevant or impractical about that.

Remember how the apostle Paul used doctrine as the basis for correct lifestyle. In Romans, a letter written to a church he had no prior involvement with, the first eleven chapters are loaded with basic Christian doctrine (sin, salvation, sanctification, eschatology). Then beginning in chapter 12, he exhorts and commands particulars necessary for godly living. We see the same order clearly in Ephesians (doctrine in chapters 1–3 and practice in 4–6) and Colossians (doctrine in chapters 1–2 and practice in 3–4) and to a less marked extent in his other letters (e.g., 1 Cor.; Phil.; 1 Thess.; 2 Thess.).

A second excuse for neglecting doctrine says that since it is difficult to understand doctrinal teaching we should not press it on people. We are admonished to "put the cookies on the lower shelf." That is good advice for some occasions and for some audiences. But think what would happen if we always followed that advice. We would produce hunchbacked Christians! Remember how babies grow. They push up on their hands and knees, then they crawl, then they try to stand up with help, and then on their own. To be on their own, they have to exercise, stretch, and reach up. So it is with Christians. To be strong we have to exercise and stretch. And to promote that process, we who teach should not always put the cookies on the lower shelf.

To be sure, some doctrines involve difficulties in understanding them. But that shouldn't keep us from trying to delve in as far as the Scriptures speak on these more complex areas. Should we soft-pedal teaching the virgin birth because we do not fully understand how it was accomplished? Or shall we ignore the summary statement of the doctrine of Christ in

1 Timothy 3:16, which includes references to his incarnation, resurrection, and ascension?[3] If, as seems likely, this was part of an early Christian hymn, then this was a part of early Christian worship. Too, other facets of the God-man, the death of Christ, and the bodily resurrection of Christ include mysteries we will never fully comprehend, but to avoid these doctrines is to starve people who need sound doctrine to feed on in order to mature.

In the area of prophecy, the perception sometimes given is that prophecy is too complicated and debated to expose people to it. Therefore, we should avoid it. But many aspects of prophecy are plain and clear. For example, Revelation 6:4 contains thirty-one words (in one English translation). Of those thirty-one words only four are two-syllable words, and one has three syllables. The other twenty-six are single-syllable words, and all of them are easily understood. The word "only begotten" in John 3:16 is much more difficult to explain than most words in prophetic passages.

Milk truth is appropriate for the infant stage of Christian growth, but solid food is necessary for maturity (Heb. 5:12–14). In that passage the writer makes clear that solid food enables the believer to use the Word to discern between good and evil. By knowing the deeper truths of the Bible, we can practice righteousness. Biblical truth—all of it—is both relevant and practical for the Christian life.[4]

A third excuse made for not emphasizing doctrine is that doctrines divide believers. That's true, but it is not a legitimate reason to avoid studying and understanding Bible doctrine. A lot of things divide churches and believers. A hot topic these days concerns different styles of worship—music, praise bands, etc. Why are there different denominations? Simply because groups understand certain teachings of the Bible differently and consider those differences significant enough to form a denomination. For example, different views of baptism, or understanding what spiritual gifts are operative today, or different types of church government reflect different interpretations of various doctrines. If divisions are wrong, then logically we should all make haste back to the Roman Catholic Church. Or actually we should try to return to the church of New Testament times. But even back then there were divisions. Immediately one thinks of the church at Corinth, which was plagued with divisions over styles of ministry (1 Cor. 1:12–13), over the basic teaching concerning bodily resurrection (1 Cor. 15), and over proper use of church discipline (2 Cor. 2:5–11). And yet the apostle Paul told the church that "there must also be factions among you, so that those who are approved may become evident among you" (1 Cor. 11:19). *Factions* means "parties who choose particular views," which will cause those who are approved by choosing the correct view to stand out from others.

Remember, too, the sharp dispute and division between Paul and Silas over whether they should take John Mark along with them on the second missionary journey (Acts 15:36–40). This resulted from a difference of opinion over the qualifications or maturity of Mark, and each "side" thought he was right. In this case God used this dispute to send out two missionary groups instead of only one.

It is not necessarily wrong to have divisions among believers. It can be but not always. And we need to remember that doctrinal differences also unite, and often that is a good thing. Our responsibility is to study, learn, teach, and preach Bible doctrine thoroughly.

Learn it and live it.

SOME REASONS DOCTRINE IS IMPORTANT (AND PRACTICAL)

Doctrine serves as the foundation for the Christian life and the motivation for Christian activity. On the doctrine of our co-crucifixion with Christ rests the call for total dedication of our lives (Rom. 6:1–13). Knowing that God does not show partiality, neither should we in respect to how we relate to rich and poor who come into the church (James 2:1–4). The hope of our Lord's return ought to purify our lives (1 John 3:3). Because of the love of Christ (his love for me and my love for him), we let our lives be controlled by him (2 Cor. 5:14). Knowing the doctrine of our future judgment, we are motivated to persuade people to receive the Lord (2 Cor. 5:10). All of these important Christian responsibilities are based on doctrinal truths.

Only by knowing the truth can we know and counter false teaching and errant living. The thirteen plus lifestyles and actions listed in 1 Timothy 1:8–10 (e.g., rebelliousness, ungodliness, lying, homosexuality) are "contrary to sound teaching."

As we approach the end of the age, it becomes increasingly important to know sound doctrine so that we do not give people what they want to hear to have their ears tickled instead of what they need to hear so that they won't be carried away from the truth of God's Word (2 Tim. 4:1–4).

To teach (indoctrinate or doctrinize) converts is a necessary component in obeying the Great Commission (Matt. 29:19).[5]

Sound doctrine is, literally, healthy doctrine; therefore, to learn, teach, and preach doctrine brings spiritual wellness and wholeness to believers. The same word used in 3 John 2 for physical health is used in the pastoral letters for spiritually healthy doctrine (1 Tim. 4:13, 16; 5:17; 2 Tim. 1:13; 4:3; Titus 1:9, 13; 2:1, 7). In light of these verses, who can dare to suggest that doctrine is not practical? Notice also that some of these verses are addressed particularly to Timothy and therefore apply especially to ministers and leaders (1 Tim. 4:13, 16; Titus 2:1, 7).

Some significant and practical ramifications stem from the importance of doctrine. First, realize that everyone has a doctrinal system, even though the individual may not realize or acknowledge this to be true. It may be systematic or unorganized, even sloppy, but we all operate on the basis of some doctrinal scheme. Obviously the "free thinking" atheist and agnostic do, as well as the more structured Calvinist and Arminian. Therefore, the preacher and teacher, professional and layman, need to read theology regardless of his type or place or level of service.

Second, never demean the importance of semantics. How often I have heard a student attempt to rationalize a poor or imprecise statement by saying, "It's just a matter of semantics." Such a response is supposed to excuse fuzzy or sloppy, if not wrong, choice of words. That student is more on target than he realizes when he says it's a matter of semantics since everything we say or write or even think concerns semantics. Semantics involves the study of meanings of words; therefore, the words we use affect the meaning we are trying to convey. So as we study, think about, teach, preach, and live the Word of God, we must pay careful attention to the words we use in communicating that they are precise, clear, and exact.

A concluding and sobering thought: what I teach today will be a part of shaping people, churches, and missions tomorrow.

Since doctrine is so important and relevant, how then can I communicate the doctrines of Scripture so that they may become implanted in our minds and hearts and displayed in our lives?

Read on.

Chapter Two

---◆---

COMMUNICATING DOCTRINE BY USING MAJOR BIBLE PASSAGES

Probably this method of teaching doctrine would be the first to come to mind since it is most obvious. "By using major Bible passages," I mean expounding the central or major passages on which a particular doctrine is based. Of course, a single passage, albeit a major one, may not develop fully all the facets of a doctrine, though a central passage will usually present a most important or basic aspect of that particular teaching. In some cases one might choose to use several major passages related to a particular doctrine in a series of studies. Also in the course of studying or teaching through a book of the Bible, one will come to a major doctrinal passage and expound it there. Certainly, one should never pass over such crucial passages or treat them superficially.

When using such passages in a teaching or preaching situation, give attention to two things that will help communicate. The first is the title. I liken the title to the gift wrap on a present. Best it not be glitzy, or cute, or too plain, but attractive and compelling to the audience so that they want to see what the package contains. My opinion is that a title that may be rather ordinary is preferable to one that is clever because the ordinary one will be more apt to be remembered. A clever title usually involves a less direct and clear expression of the text, and although the cute title might be remembered, the text may not be. Nevertheless, having said that, it is true that a clever title may draw clear attention to the text and at the same time be memorable.

Second, when the package (passage) is opened, then the hearer will expect to be greeted by an introduction that will show the importance of correctly understanding the doctrine. Sometimes such an introduction can be taken from the religion section of the newspaper or what some radio or television preacher has said recently—or from some book. From such sources the best kind of quote would be a heretical statement or explanation of the doctrine. The contrast between the error quoted and the truth about to be expounded will grab the listener's attention and (if recent or from some well-known person) will demonstrate that the heresy is being promoted right now and in the place we live. In turn this will stress the importance of knowing the truth as well as exposing the false teaching. If the heresy is being taught by someone who is prominent in the public eye, then exposing it ought to warn the audience not to support the person or his ministry in any way, especially not financially.

At the time I was writing this chapter, the local paper published a major article about a well-known televangelist. The article raised serious questions about his lack of financial responsibility and integrity and also reported some of the man's strange teachings. Among them were these: "God originally intended women to give birth from their sides; Adam was able to fly; and the Holy Trinity was not one divine entity but three, each with a body, mind and spirit."[1] In particular the heretical statement about the Trinity would serve as a great introduction to teach the truth about the Trinity. Indeed, a pastor would do well to interrupt whatever series he might be in to explain the orthodox statement of the Trinity while the article was still fresh in people's minds.

Contrary to what seems to be the custom these days, there may be occasions when one would do better to plunge directly into the biblical text and let the context serve as the introduction (in such instances one could be certain that the introduction was inerrant!). Indeed, I fear that contemporary homiletics (the art of preaching) too often attempts to pour students into a straightjacket of sermon structure. They are told that it is essential to have a grabber at the beginning to gain the audience's attention before launching into the biblical text. H. A. Ironside, who was known and acknowledged as "the prince of preachers," almost always began his messages by inviting his listeners "to turn to" [his text]. Often his introduction would consist of the background of the passage to be explained. Even the great C. H. Spurgeon did not consistently begin with a grabber. Is it too outlandish or naïve to think that ideally our audiences might mature to the place where they are "grabbed" by the simple fact that they are going to open their Bibles to see and hear what God says?

Before turning to some examples of major doctrinal passages, I want to urge pastors and leaders of churches and organizations that have a doctrinal statement to expose their people to the exposition and understanding of that statement on a regular basis. Certainly new converts and those joining the church need to be taught the truths that the group holds and promotes. Even longtime members need to be reminded and refreshed about the doctrine of the group. It is far too easy to forget and/or slight the importance of that for which the church stands. The same holds true for parachurch organizations whose members need to be reminded of what the organization believes and proclaims.

Here are some examples (not necessarily fully developed) of this approach to healthy doctrinal communication.

THE DOCTRINE OF GIVING

Title: "To Give or Not to Give? Here Is the Answer." Or, "Grace Giving." Or (if you are brave enough!) "Does God Require the Tithe Today?"

Text: 2 Corinthians 8–9 (and/or 1 Cor. 16:2). The longer passage may require more than one session while the shorter one could be used separately if only one session is available.

Introduction: Reports of the percentage of income Christians of various groups' giving appear in the media regularly. Before election times candidates often make public their income tax statements. Those tax statements of our government officials reveal the amount of their giving and its percentage of their income. A recent statistic revealed that church members on average give only 2.3 percent of their income to the church.

If you use 1 Corinthians 16:2, the verse says three things about grace giving: when to give (on Sunday), the mechanics (put aside and save; i.e., designate an amount each week to be segregated into a personal fund from which fund distributions are made), and how much (in proportion to God's prospering). The last point requires detailed explanation, including such matters as the number of tithes required under the Mosaic Law and for what purposes they were required, whether tithing is the standard for today, and a reminder to those with larger incomes that the proportion (that is, the percentage of their income) should increase, which, of course, will increase the dollar amount.[2]

If you use 2 Corinthians 8–9, here is a suggested basic (and alliterated!) outline.

1. Principles for Giving (8:1–6)
2. Purposes for Giving (8:7–15)
3. Policies in Giving (8:16–24)
4. Promises for Giving (9:6–15)

Years ago I was listening to a group of missionaries in a poor country discussing how they could teach their people to tithe, which would have been considerably more than they were able to give at that time. Eventually I spoke up and urged them to teach the people to give proportionately, since the day might well come when that country would prosper and giving only a tithe would be less than they should give. Regrettably I have heard pastors in my country figure 10 percent of the average income of their parishioners as the solution for all the church's needs. But some members should be giving more (sometimes much more) than 10 percent. While for others in financial straits, 10 percent would be more than God expects.

THE DOCTRINE OF JUSTIFICATION

Text: Romans 3:21–26

Title: "How Good Does a Person Have to Be to Get to Heaven?"

Introduction: Point out the confusion over the meaning of *justification* and emphasize the fact that justification is one of the most important and often misunderstood doctrines of the Bible. If the setting is appropriate, ask the audience either to write or to verbalize a definition of justification.

Justification concerns righteousness, but when used to explain how an individual can be righteous in God's sight, confusion takes over. The Roman Catholic doctrine of justification declares that righteousness is infused through a gradual process into one's life. Some Protestant writers say that to justify is to *make* the sinner righteous, rather than to *declare* the sinner righteous. If one were to take a random survey asking how a person can be right before God, many, I suspect, would respond by saying that good works will justify. Therefore, it is of utmost importance when discussing this subject to keep emphasizing that to *justify* means "to declare (not make) righteous."

A simpler introduction could use a quote that bases justification on good works.

Highlights in Developing the Passage

1. The Problem. Read Job 9:2b: "How can a man be righteous before God?" (NKJV). The answer to Job's question and that of the title is that to get to heaven one has to be as good as Jesus Christ. How then can anyone ever hope to be in heaven?

2. God's Plan to Solve the Problem (Rom. 3:21–25). God's righteousness is given to us through faith in Christ's propitiatory (satisfactory) sacrifice and as a free gift.

3. The Pronouncement That Declares Us Righteous (Rom. 3:26).[3]

THE DOCTRINE OF THE KENOSIS

Title: "What Happened When Our Lord Became Man"

Text: Philippians 2:5–8

Introduction: I suggest highlighting the difficulty of stating this doctrine by asking some questions: "Did our Lord lose or compromise his deity at his incarnation?" (The answer: no.) "Did our Lord lack anything we associate with humanity?" (The answer: yes—a sin nature.)

Emphases in Developing the Passage

Of necessity, if one plans faithfully to expose the teaching of this passage, there will have to be a discussion of important words and phrases in the section. These will include "existed in the form of God" (v. 5a), "equality . . . a thing to be grasped" (v. 6), "emptied" (v. 7), and "humbled" (v. 8), "bond-servant" (v. 7), "likeness" (v. 7), and "appearance" (v. 9). Perhaps it would be helpful to read appropriate sections of the Chalcedonian Creed (AD 451).

Verse 5, as elaborated in verses 1–4 and exemplified in our Lord, serves as the practical ramification of the kenosis, namely, let believers unite in selfless service to others.

THE DOCTRINE OF GENERAL REVELATION

Text: Psalm 19:1–6

Title: "Star Gazing"

Introduction: Include some facts about the number of stars we can see (only around 3,000, although the Milky Way contains 200 billion). Also briefly discuss the meaning of *revelation* and the difference between general and special revelation. In this Psalm creation is the channel of the revelation of the glory of God.

A Suggested Outline

1. The Continuousness of the Revelation of God's Glory in Creation (the tenses in vv. 1–2)
2. The Clarity of This Revelation—Nonverbal yet Clear (v. 3)
3. The Coverage of This Revelation—Everywhere the Sun Can Be Seen or Felt (vv. 4–6)

Conclusion: What we see and feel each day and night ought to make us ask, "How did the universe come into existence?" And the answer can lead to an evangelistic appeal.

Other doctrines and their central passages should easily come to mind. Examples include each of the attributes of God, the original sin of man (Gen. 3:1–7), imputation (Rom. 5:12–21), qualifications for church leaders (1 Tim. 3:1–13), and judgment of believers (1 Cor. 3:10–15). Some will be part of the sequential exposition of a book in the Bible. Others will be used alone. The exposition of a single central passage is the method suggested in this chapter. When several passages are involved to teach a doctrine (e.g., inspiration of the Bible), this is the approach of systematic theology, which we look at next.[4]

Chapter Three

---◆---

COMMUNICATING DOCTRINE BY USING SYSTEMATIC THEOLOGY

At a board meeting of a well-known Christian institution, the devotional speaker had emphasized the importance of preaching the Bible. It was a stirring message and an important reminder. An hour or so later, one board member (who had heard the message) prayed that the institution would always preach the Bible and not be sidetracked onto "peripheral [his word] matters of doctrine and theology." An oxymoronic prayer, to say the least!

Yet it is a prayer, or at least a thought, that too many evangelicals would agree with. Why? Possibly because they do not understand what doctrine and theology are all about, or they do not realize that doctrine forms the warp and woof of solid biblical preaching.

Theology is the study of God. Literally the word means "a word about God." For the Christian that means the study of the living and true God. Of course, theologies exist of the gods of false religions. Systematic theology is distinct from biblical theology, historical theology, or philosophical theology. Actually the sources for systematic theology can include all the ways God reveals himself. What is generally called "natural revelation," that is, the revelation of God through nature, belongs under the umbrella of systematic theology. But the content of natural theology is limited, though real and purposeful. Too, the experiences people have that purport to reveal something about God could be part of the material of systematic theology. However, such experiences cannot be guaranteed not to be spurious. So the data of systematic theology that we can consider absolutely truthful come from the Bible. And certainly the Bible contains enough data for many lifetimes of investigation.

So the first step in using systematic theology to communicate doctrine involves collecting information. Second, this data needs to be interpreted and clearly understood so that there is no doubt about its being appropriate to the subject being investigated. Then, third, follows the process of systematizing the relevant material, which will include evaluating, prioritizing, arranging, and wrapping up the results in a neat package. A more formal definition of systematic theology, which includes the steps above, might be this: systematic theology is the correlation of biblical information as a whole in order to explain and exhibit systematically the total material of various aspects of God's revelation.

Of course, a relationship exists between the central passages (considered in the preceding chapter) and the material of systematic theology. For example, the doctrine of giving, while having an obvious central passage (2 Cor. 8–9), also has other relevant passages: Matthew 6:1–4, 19–24; Luke 6:38; 12:13–21; 1 Corinthians 16:2; 1 Timothy 6:6–10; Hebrews 13:5; and James 2:1–4; 5:2–6. Studying and teaching the doctrine of giving would require consideration of all these passages, which together with the central passage constitute the doctrine of giving from the viewpoint of systematic theology.

Often when systematic theology is mentioned, two objections arise. One is that systematic theology is too dry to be useful. We wouldn't want to say that the material (i.e., God's truth) is dry, so if theology is dry, the fault must be with the communicator. At the same time, certain teachings in the Bible will admittedly be of more interest to some than other things, which may involve factors like the reader's background, personality, or spiritual maturity or immaturity. Nevertheless, the student and teacher must strive to correlate and exhibit the material in an attractive manner, always being conscious that theological terminology and customary labels may need to be more clearly defined, even changed or updated. I do not subscribe to the idea that we should abandon good terms for poorer ones just because people are not acquainted with the better ones. Yet temporarily one may have to use different terms and labels instead of the standard ones simply because the audience is unfamiliar with any terms. But these should be temporary. Sometimes we need to stretch our hearers' minds. "Dry" may be the fault of the communicator, or it may be the result of the reader's or hearer's resistance to stretch, think, and learn new words and concepts.

Once while having a Bible study with a group of swimmers at a university, I quickly came to realize they had no clue as to the meaning of customary terms simply because almost all of them had no previous exposure to the Bible. And yet they wanted to learn about the future (eschatology). So when I taught them about what we correctly call the rapture, I substituted the phrase "the big snatch." The period of the coming tribulation became "big trouble." The millennium was "utopia." These labels I felt were legitimate for that audience temporarily, but as individual members of the group grew in biblical understanding, then we reverted to the biblical terms. And, of course *rapture, tribulation,* and *millennium* are biblical terms, the underlying meanings of which describe the event or period involved. Therefore, using these biblical labels helps the learner remember what the doctrine means. *Rapture* means "to be caught up," and the rapture of the church will be just that. *Tribulation* means "a time of trouble," which it certainly will be. And the word *millennium* expresses the length of that future time.

A second objection tars systematic theology with irrelevance. If this be true and if material for systematic theology comes from the Bible, then one would be forced to conclude that the material in the Bible is irrelevant. Though objectors would not want to admit that, this is what they are implying. Granted the presentation might be or seem to be irrelevant, but that is not the fault of the biblical material. More likely the problem would lie in the structure and/or presentation of the material. Relevance can often be established in the introduction to the subject either by citing errors people know something about or by relating to the interests the hearers have. For example, just relating to areas of theology, an introduction might cite errors in the authority and or interpretation of the Bible or in the man in the street's concept of God, or who Jesus is, or different conceptions of the Holy Spirit. Interests that people have include ideas about Satan and/or demons, what they think the church is and what it should be doing, or what will happen in the future.

A word of caution: relevance should never be forced either by suggesting some application that is not in the biblical text or by restricting relevance to what I may think the hearers need. The preacher/teacher must never forget that the Holy Spirit knows the needs of every person listening and knows them better than I do, and in most cases better than the hearer thinks he or she knows them. After all, the Holy Spirit knows everything, and we do not. Too, we must never forget that the Spirit can use a verse or passage to reach someone in a manner which we could not imagine. Our prepared application of the text may easily be too forced, too limited, or too useless for some of those listening.

Some time ago I taught a Bible class for three months in a home in the Philadelphia area; the studies were in the book of Ephesians. One evening I was invited to dinner before class in the home of one of the members. When I arrived, the hostess took me aside to tell me that a friend of hers would be at dinner and class. This friend lived about one hundred miles from Philadelphia, had left her home and husband, and sought refuge in the home of the hostess. In other words she was beginning the process that she wanted to lead to divorce from her husband (both were unsaved).

Can you guess what passage in Ephesians was scheduled for that evening? Yes, Ephesians 5:22–33, which concerns husband-wife relationships. I had been consistently teaching through Ephesians, so to interrupt the sequence or change the subject entirely would have been disruptive. What should I do? The question had completely killed my appetite for the excellent dinner. But I finally decided to go ahead as scheduled. The lady came. I taught Ephesians 5:22–33. I went home second-guessing what I had done. I had no idea how the lady reacted to what she heard.

No idea until several weeks later when the hostess told me the rest of the story. The hostess led her friend to the Lord that week; the lady returned home to her husband; and after a month or so the husband also came to Christ. Never underestimate what the Holy Spirit will do with a Scripture that may seem inappropriate or irrelevant to us but which he can take and use in ways we could never imagine.

Here are some examples of using systematic theology to communicate doctrine.

THE DOCTRINE OF THE HOLY SPIRIT

Using as complete as possible a correlation of the biblical material on the Holy Spirit, one would need a series to cover the subject in any reasonable depth.

Texts: Many, but choose a key one to begin the message.

Introduction: Perhaps a quote (not difficult to find) from some theologian or commentator who denies the reality of the Holy Spirit. Or perhaps refer to excesses about the Spirit often heard on TV.

Some Suggestions for Developing the Subject

I. The Holy Spirit—It or He?
   A. He is a person (personality).
   B. He is God (deity).

II. The Holy Spirit—Where Is He?
   A. He is in the world (omnipresence).
   B. He is in the believer (indwelling).

III. The Holy Spirit—What Is He Doing Today?
   A. He makes our gospel preaching clear—conviction (John 16:8–11).
   B. He effects the new birth—regeneration (John 3:1–16).
   C. He joins us to the body of Christ—baptizing (1 Cor. 12:13).
   D. He secures our salvation—sealing (Eph. 4:30).
   E. He desires to control our lives (Eph. 5:18).
   F. He gives us spiritual gifts—gifting (Rom. 12; 1 Cor. 12; Eph. 4).
   G. He helps out praying (Rom. 8:25; Eph. 6:18).
   H. He teaches (John 16:13–14).
   I. He exhorts local churches (Rev. 2–3).

IV. Can Anyone Commit the Unpardonable Sin (Matt. 12:24–37)?
   Hopefully you will be brave enough to tackle this subject

since many people are confused about it and concerned, thinking they may have committed it.

THE DOCTRINE OF THE HOLY SPIRIT

Another approach to this same doctrine focuses on Ephesians as the basis for a series.

Text: Verses from the book of Ephesians.

Title: "What the Holy Spirit Does and What He Expects from Churches" (remember Ephesians was a circular letter to churches in Asia Minor).

Development: You will need to start by looking up *Spirit* in a concordance to be certain you include all the references to the Spirit in Ephesians.

I. What He Does for Us
   A. He seals believers (1:13; 4:30).
   B. He is the pledge of our inheritance (1:14).
   C. He opens access to the Father (2:18).
   D. He unites us to God (2:22).
   E. He gives us understanding of the mystery (3:5–6).
   F. He strengthens us (3:16).

II. What He Expects of Us
   A. He expects us to keep his unity (4:3).
   B. He expects us to use his spiritual gifts (4:11).
   C. He expects us not to grieve him by our speech (4:29–31).
   D. He expects us to be filled with the Spirit (5:18).
   E. He expects us to use the sword of the Spirit (6:17).
   F. He expects us to pray in the Spirit (6:18).

THE DOCTRINE OF SATAN

Texts: Many, but choose a significant/familiar one to begin.

Title: "What's in a Name?" Rather than trying to cover all the Scripture teaches about Satan, you could just approach the subject by the various names Satan has.

List of Names of Satan

1. Satan the Serpent (Gen. 3:1; Rev. 12:9)
2. Satan the Tempter (Acts 5; 1 Thess. 3:5; 1 Cor. 7:5)
3. Satan the Ruler of This World (John 12:31)
4. Satan the Roaring Lion (1 Pet. 5:8)
5. Satan the Adversary (Matt. 4:10; Rev. 12:10)
6. Satan the Church Worker
   - In the church at Corinth (2 Cor. 2:11)
   - In the church at Smyrna (Rev. 2:9)
   - In the church at Pergamum (Rev. 2:1)
   - In the church at Thyatira (Rev. 2:24)

This list of names may well require a series, but the relevance and application of these names will come easily and pointedly.

Preparation for teaching from the viewpoint of systematic theology ought to begin with reading the related section(s) in a good systematic theology book. Supplement and develop this basic material by using a concordance and commentaries.

An important (exceedingly relevant today) reminder from the great preacher, Charles Haddon Spurgeon.

Be well instructed in theology, and do not regard the sneers of those who rail at it because they are ignorant of it. Many preachers are not theologians, and hence

the mistakes which they make. It cannot do any hurt
to the most lively evangelist to be also a sound theologian, and it may often be the means of saving him from
gross blunders. Nowadays, we hear men tear a single
sentence of Scripture from its connection, and cry
"Eureka! Eureka!" as if they had found a new truth;
and yet they have not discovered a diamond, but a
piece of broken glass. . . . Let us be thoroughly well
acquainted with the great doctrines of the Word of
God.[1]

Similarly, in my student days one of my revered professors,
Lewis Sperry Chafer, an eminent theologian, exhorted us by
saying, "Would that theologians were also evangelists, and
would that evangelists were also theologians." He was, though
not many are.

Chapter Four

———◆———

COMMUNICATING
DOCTRINE FROM THE
PERSPECTIVE OF BIBLICAL
THEOLOGY

What is biblical theology? How does it differ from systematic theology? And how can it be used to preach and teach doctrine engagingly? These are significant questions to ask and answer before using the method.

WHAT IS BIBLICAL THEOLOGY?

When the average person hears the term *biblical theology*, I suspect he or she thinks it means "a theology based on the Bible." In other words, biblical theology in this view is differentiated from philosophical theology, which is not primarily based on the Bible. Sometimes the rather generic term *biblical theology* means the theology of the apostolic age, and sometimes it means "the history of doctrine throughout the church period." Some consider biblical theology as doctrine presented more popularly rather than academically.

Here is my definition of *biblical theology*: it is that aspect of theology which deals systematically with the historically conditioned progress of the revelation of God as found in the Bible. Let's dissect that definition.

Systematically. The results of studying the Bible from a biblical theological perspective will be presented systematically, not haphazardly. This is not unique to biblical theology since all other approaches to theology (whether philosophical, pietistic, historical, or exegetical) should be presented systematically.

Historically conditioned. This feature does distinguish biblical theology from other theological approaches. Biblical theology pays careful attention to the fact that God's revelation was embodied in history. It puts the authors' flesh and blood on their writings while never forcing or overemphasizing their individualities and interests but always recognizing their writings to be under the complete superintendence of the Holy Spirit. It also views the writings in their historical setting. Investigating the background and lives of the various writers of Scripture, the circumstances which compelled them to write, and the historical situations of the recipients will greatly aid our understanding of its truth and result in an engaging way to present it.

Progress of the Revelation of God. Also a distinguishing feature of biblical theology, the progressiveness of God's revelation occupies a significant place in this approach. Obviously the Bible was not dropped out of heaven, beautifully bound with gilt edges, and in the canonical order of the books! One must recognize that what we now have as completed revelation came in stages, in differing amounts, to different men, and in different periods of human history. The revelation of God was not completed in one act but involved a long series of successive acts through the minds and hands of many human authors who had varying backgrounds. Biblical theology studies the Word of God in the way in which it was written—progressively.

In the Bible. The source for the study of biblical theology is the Bible. This is not to say that facts and insights from other sources are entirely ruled out, but it affirms that the doctrine to be systematized is found in the words of the Bible. Even biblical theologians who do not hold a high view of inspiration nevertheless attempt to build their biblical theology on biblical revelation, though often interpreted through liberal glasses.

HOW DOES BIBLICAL THEOLOGY COMPARE TO SYSTEMATIC THEOLOGY?

Though similarities exist between biblical theology and systematic theology, there also are similarities as well as distinguishing features. Similarities include the following: Both disciplines are biblical. Both are systematic. Both are (or should be) based on the Bible. Nevertheless some differences also exist. Biblical theology investigates the various writers, times, recipients, and process that went into the writing of the Scriptures. It spotlights the progress in giving God's revelation. It gives us the records of revelation in process. On the other hand, systematic theology concerns the finished product.

In gathering material for the study of these two approaches, biblical theology concentrates on a particular author through whom revelation came or a particular period of time when it was given. Systematic theology gathers material on a particular teaching from all parts of the Bible. For example, from a biblical theology viewpoint, the doctrine of inspiration may be presented from James's teaching in his letter. From a systematic theology perspective, the doctrine of inspiration will use passages from several portions of the Bible in constructing the doctrine. Sometimes a study can combine biblical and systematic theology as illustrated in the preceding chapter with the work of the Holy Spirit in Ephesians.

WHAT USE DOES BIBLICAL THEOLOGY MAKE OF OTHER STUDIES?

The study of biblical theology must include matters related to Old and New Testament introduction—authorship, date of writing, and destination, for example. These help give the historical perspective so necessary to biblical theology. Did Paul write the Pastoral Epistles? The answer makes a major difference as to whether these three letters are included in Pauline theology. Or, who were the intended readers of Hebrews?

The use of good exegesis is paramount in the study of biblical theology just as it is in systematic theology and every other use of the Bible. Poor or inadequate interpretation results in poor theology. One cannot be a theologian without being an exegete, though one can be an exegete without being a theologian.

Hopefully the concept and methodology of biblical theology is clear enough to proceed with examples of its use in studying and communicating doctrine. Here are a few.

THE DOCTRINE OF INSPIRATION IN JAMES

Title: "An Apostle's View of the Bible" or

"What Christ's Half Brother Thought about the Bible"

Introduction: Landmarks in the life of James: in family of at least seven siblings, an unbeliever until Christ's resurrection, leader in the church in Jerusalem, different from the other Jameses mentioned in the New Testament.

Suggestions: Emphasize the godliness of the home in which James was reared. Note his mother Mary's knowledge of the Old Testament. There are fifteen discernable quotations from the Old Testament in her Magnificat (Luke 1:46–56). Note also James's use of Scripture in his short letter which contains 108 verses. James alludes to Scriptures from twenty-two books of the Old Testament. In addition he uses fifteen allusions to Jesus' teaching (as exemplified in the Sermon on the Mount).

To capture James's view and use of the Word of God in a neat package, here is a suggested way to do it.

1. James's Attitude toward the Word
    a. It is truth (1:18).
    b. It is Scripture (4:5–6). Scripture was a specific term to refer to the Old Testament and not to other Jewish literature. Therefore, it is authoritative.
2. James's Application of the Word
    a. It is the means of regeneration (1:18, 21).
    b. Like a mirror it reflects the defects of men (1:23–25).
    c. It is a guide for living (2:8).
    d. It will serve as a standard for future judgment (2:12).

Conclusion: It is not enough to acknowledge the authority of the Word and the usefulness of the Word. We must also be doers of the Word (1:22).

WHAT JESUS BELIEVED

I have found that a series on what Jesus believed or taught about various subjects to have a built-in attraction simply because it has to do with Jesus (and some people still seem to think that what's in red letters is more inspired than what is in black letters!). I have used this series in home Bible classes as well as in churches. It can be easily shortened or lengthened to suit the allotted time.

This kind of approach is a good example of biblical theology because it surfaces Jesus' thoughts about various subjects, and the subjects he deals with usually grow out of a historical or cultural setting, which needs to be an integral part of the explanation. Of course, one must consult a concordance to be sure that no related passage has been overlooked.

Here are some relevant and easily applied subjects that could be included in such a series.

What Jesus taught about . . .

1. Himself
2. His Bible
3. Sin
4. Forgiveness
5. Prayer
6. Money
7. The Future

And other subjects that will come to mind as you study this concept. As examples, consider these.

Title: "What Jesus Taught about Money"

Introduction: Brokers, financial planners, estate consultants abound (and they all are pricey!). Listen carefully to what financial planner Lord Jesus freely advises about money.

Suggestions: This topic may lend itself to be developed and expressed in propositional statements rather than using a word or phrase outline.

Development

I. Either poverty or riches can be a blessing (Luke 6:20; 8:3).

II. Riches may keep one from entering the kingdom (Matt. 13:22; 19:16–22). Illustrations of this principle.

    A. The wealthy young ruler (Matt. 19:15–22)

    B. The rich fool (Luke 12:16–21)

    C. The rich man (Luke 16:19–31)

III. Money can breed greed (Luke 12:12–15).

IV. Money should be used to prepare for a rewarded future (Luke 16:9).

V. People should work, work hard, and work shrewdly (Luke 19:11–27; 16:1–8).

VI. All should give.

    A. Give even if poor (Mark 12:43).

    B. Give generously (Luke 6:38).

    C. Give privately (Matt. 6:2–4).

VII. Money can prevent one from a full commitment to the Lord.

    A. The principle (Matt. 6:19–24)

    B. The warning (Luke 14:25–33)

Conclusion: "A man's life does not consist in the abundance of his possessions" (Luke 12:15).

Title: What Jesus Believed about the Bible

I. What was Jesus' Bible? Luke 11:51 sets the limits from Genesis (Abel, Gen. 4:8) to 2 Chronicles (Zech. 14:20), which was the last book in the order of the Hebrew Bible. Note that he does not include any of the martyrs mentioned in the Apocrypha, which indicates that he did not place the Apocrypha on the same level as the canonical books.[1] He also preauthenticated the writings of the New Testament (John 14:26).

II. What were Jesus' attitudes toward his Bible?

    A. He believed it was accurate to its very details. Carefully exegete Matthew 4:4; 5:18; 22:32.

    B. He believed it was historically reliable. Examples include these.

       1. The account and historicity of Adam and Eve (Matt. 19:3–5)

       2. The flood in Noah's time (Luke 17:26–27)

       3. The destruction of Sodom (Luke 17:28–29)

       4. The account of Jonah and the great fish (Matt. 12:40)

       5. The historicity of Isaiah (Matt. 12:17); Elijah (Matt. 17:11–12); Abel (Matt. 23:35); Abiathar (Mark 2:26); David (Matt. 22:45); Moses and his writings (Matt. 8:4; John 5:46); Abraham, Isaac, Jacob (Matt. 8:11; John 8:39)

    C. He believed that he fulfilled certain Old Testament passages (Luke 4:21; 24:25–27).

    D. He believed that the words of the Bible were true and practical (Matt. 4:1–11).

III. What conclusions do we need to draw for ourselves?

    A. We cannot call ourselves full followers of Jesus without having the same attitudes toward the Bible that he did. This includes trusting its historical accuracy and all its details.

    B. Though we will never know the Bible as well as he did, we must seek to know it as well as we can.

    C. We can use it for doctrine (Matt. 22:41–46), rebuke (Matt. 22:31), correction (Matt. 15:7–9), and instruction in righteousness (John 17:17; see 2 Tim. 3:16).

Fellowship According to John

Title: "What Is Biblical Fellowship?" Or, "Fellowship Is More Than Coffee and Doughnuts"

Text: Selected passages in 1 John

Introduction: One of the characteristics of the earliest days of the church was fellowship (Acts 2:42). Define *fellowship* as "sharing or having in common" (resist using "two men in a ship"). If anyone would know what fellowship means, it would be the apostle John who walked with our Lord while he was on earth and who lived and labored the longest of all the apostles. In 1 John he develops the subject in depth (1 John 1:1–3).

Development

  I. Conditions for Having Fellowship
   A. Walk in the light (1:7). This is a progressive, developing, ever-widening concept that can never be completely achieved in this life.
   B. Confess sin when we find areas of darkness (1:9).

 II. The Characteristics of Being in Fellowship
   A. Practicing righteousness (3:4–9).
   B. Loving one another (3:10–18).

III. Conduct When One Is in Fellowship
   A. Imitate the life of Christ (2:1–11).
   B. Separate from the world (2:12–17).
   C. Do not listen to false teachings of Antichrists (2:18–29).

Conclusion: Make an appointment regularly to meet, listen to, and obey the living and true God (Amos 3:3).

Although it may take some acclimatizing to the environment of biblical theology, it is well worth the effort, for it brings a dimension to the study and teaching of doctrine that in some ways makes it more meaningful and down to earth. The biblical theology approach can personalize the text by making the reader feel more attached and related to the writers and their writings with their varying emphases.

Chapter Five

———◆———

TEACHING DOCTRINE FROM A CONCORDANCE

A study of any number of words and/or phrases in a concordance will yield a gold mine of material for learning, preaching, and teaching doctrines. These will not always fall into the category of major doctrines though some will; for example, the doctrine of redemption can easily be built on the three major words used. But other doctrines can fill important gaps left by only teaching the major ones. They also speak to many facets of the Christian life that might otherwise be overlooked.

If you know Greek and/or Hebrew, then by all means use a concordance based on the original words and not on a translation. If you use an English concordance, remember that English translations often use different English words to translate the same Greek or Hebrew word. You need to discover all the uses of the original word by using the numbering system that English concordances use. It is crucial to investigate every word related to the particular doctrine. However, you may not need to use every reference. You will likely combine some, eliminate some, and focus on certain ones only.

The proliferation of English translations requires using a concordance based on the particular translation. Also, when teaching or preaching, wisdom dictates discovering which translation will be in the hands of the audience. If no single translation is used by most of the hearers, then be sure to note different ways the word or phrase you are presenting is translated in several translations being used by the audience. Otherwise, when you read a verse that uses the word you are studying, but a different translation uses a different word, listeners may think they have the wrong reference. Also, in the presentation of the message, try to avoid turning to too many passages, or you will lose the audience. Ask them to turn to the more important ones, and you can read others for them without their turning to them.

First and foremost, however, have a correct definition of the word(s) on which the doctrine is based. Do not necessarily be satisfied with the meaning translators choose to translate the word, but look up definitions in Greek, Hebrew, and English dictionaries. And remember, a definition must be basic enough to explain the word wherever the word is used in the text. The meaning may have to be narrowed in some uses, but the basic meaning cannot be violated, adjusted, or disappear.

Here are some suggestions and examples of this approach.

DON'T LOSE HEART

Title: "Hang in There!"

Texts: Six passages which use *ekkakeō* and *egkakeō* (variously translated "faint," "weary," "lose heart").

Introduction: Define the word. It involves a mental (not physical) disinclination to be faithful especially in the routines of the Christian life. "Lose heart" is the best translation.

Illustrate the idea in other areas of life—work, study, getting up in the morning, and chores.

A Suggested Outline

1. Don't lose heart in problems (2 Cor. 4:16; Eph 3:13). What were Paul's circumstances when he wrote Ephesians? Confinement under house arrest in Rome waiting for his trial before Caesar, which certainly gave him every reason to lose heart.

2. Don't lose heart in praying (Luke 18:1). Use the illustration the Lord uses in this passage about the widow and the unjust judge (literally, "the judge of unrighteousness," v. 6).

3. Don't lose heart in performing good deeds (Gal. 6:9; 2 Thess. 3:13). Note the problems at Thessalonica, which called for Paul's exhortation. Especially note the priority of recipients of good deeds in Galatians 6:10. The application of these verses is contemporary and obvious.

4. Don't lose heart in proclaiming the gospel (2 Cor. 4:1).[1]

VAIN AND EMPTY

Title: "Happy New and All Year"

Text: Selected verses which use *kenos* (vain).

Introduction: State the meaning of the word: "empty, without content, basis, truth, power, result, goal, purpose, or profit." Perhaps hold up a ledger sheet which shows profit-and-loss columns. Or perhaps use some statistics concerning how many people feel their lives are empty. Or explain how to distinguish between the things in our lives that are useless or unprofitable and those that are useful and profitable.

Development: It would not be possible or prudent to try to include all the biblical references. You will have to select categories to discuss and divide the message into two major parts.

  I. Things without Profit
- A. A false gospel (Col. 2:1–10)
- B. Vain or empty talk (Eph. 5:6)
- C. Backsliding (1 Thess. 3:5)
- D. An empty testimony (Phil. 2:15–16)

 II. Things with Profit
- A. The true gospel attested to by a Christlike life (1 Cor. 15:1–11)
- B. Hard work for the Lord (1 Cor. 15:58)

HOW TO BE A TERRIFIC CHRISTIAN

Text: The only three passages in the New Testament where *huperekperisseuō* occurs (Eph. 3:20; 1 Thess. 3:10; 5:13).

Introduction: Superlatives are so overused that they lose any force they might have (supermarket, Super Bowl, Superman). If God used superlatives in the Bible, then we should pay attention, especially this one since he used it so few times.

Development: Explain how a prepositional prefix on a Greek word intensifies the meaning of the word. Then move to Luke 15:17 where the uncompounded word, *perisseuō*, occurs. Explain ways it is translated to convey its full meaning (e.g., "more than enough"). Then proceed to Romans 5:20 where the word is heightened and intensified with the prefix *huper*. Then try to conceive of the meaning (and an appropriate translation) when the word is doubly compounded with two prepositions (*huper* and *ek*). Perhaps we could try to convey the meaning by a doubly compounded English phrase, such as "super, super abundantly."

1. Super, Super Abundant Power (Eph. 3:20). What an encouraging promise for our praying!
2. Super, Super Abundant Prayer (1 Thess. 3:10). What an example for our praying!
3. Super, Super Abundant Esteem (1 Thess. 5:13). What an exhortation for church members!

Conclusion: If you want to be a terrific Christian, tap into the power of God, pray with the intensity Paul exemplified, and esteem highly the leadership of your church.

Here are some additional examples of significant doctrines that relate to a particular word, though I have not tried to give detailed development of these words. Hopefully they will quicken your thinking and motivate you to study and develop them adequately.

What God says to males in particular. This is built on the Greek word *anēr*. In my concordance there are three columns of uses of this word, so obviously one will have to be selective. This is a great message or series of messages for a men's retreat. Be careful not to use a gender-neutral translation, or the points will be lost.

True biblical perfection built on the Greek word teleios. Use both the adjective and the verb forms of the word and select references that concern the maturity of the believer. Contrast the biblical teaching with the perfectionism taught by some Christian groups.

Should a Christian be afraid? This constitutes a study of the New Testament teaching on fear. Three words are involved in this study, and two of them are translated variously. The first is *deilia* translated in 2 Timothy 1:7 "timidity." The second is *eulambanō* translated in Hebrews 11:7 "reverence." The third is the most often used one, *phobos*, translated "fear" in, for example, 1 Peter 1:17. All three words must be carefully defined and distinguished from one another. Don't confuse your hearers by reciting several English words used to translate them; rather focus and use one English word for each of the Greek words and imprint that word on the listeners' minds. Remember that the three verses cited above are not the only ones to use in expounding this doctrine. With *phobos* many verses must come into play in order to display this kind of fear.

The answer to the question in the title (Should a Christian be afraid?) is yes and no. We need to be afraid in certain relationships but must not be in others. This serves as a good conclusion, for it summarizes, reinforces, and applies the entire message.

What is fruit? or how to be a fruitful Christian. When you use a concordance to look up the uses of *fruit*, you will discover five specific things that are designated fruit in the Bible.

1. A developing Christian character (Gal. 5:22–23; 2 Pet. 1:5–8)
2. A life of good works (Col. 1:10; Phil. 1:22)
3. Those who come to Christ through our witness (Rom. 1:13; 1 Cor. 16:15)
4. Giving praise to God and thankfully confessing his name (Heb. 13:15)
5. Giving money to the Lord's work (Rom. 15:28; Phil. 4:17)

Make clear that these are clearly biblical fruits in contrast to lists of fruits we often create to which we insist people conform. Also be encouraging in showing that all believers can surely bear some (if not all) of the five above and therefore live a fruitful life.

If you wanted to develop a series on fruitfulness, the above would be one message and another one would surely have to be John 15:1–17. Further expansion of such a series could well include a message on being unfruitful as stated in Matthew 13:22; Titus 3:14; and 2 Peter 1:8 with corollary passages that relate to loss of rewards (1 Cor. 3:15; 2 Cor. 5:10; 2 John 8).

A list of additional doctrines that can be built on concordance studies goes on and on. If you run out, just thumb through the concordance and let your eyes fall almost anywhere for ideas.

As I was writing this, I thought I should practice what I was suggesting. So I spent about fifteen minutes in a concordance (on the King James Version). Here are some words which would lend themselves to doctrinal development.

Earthquake

Finish

Keep (in Proverbs)

Mourn (in New Testament)

Predestinate (there are only six references)

Prosper, prosperity

Prudent (in Proverbs)

Temperance

Warn, warning

Now you carry on.

Chapter Six

———◆———

Teaching Doctrine from Biblical Illustrations

By this approach I do not mean using illustrations within a message to illuminate a passage or a point but rather starting with an illustration and then moving to the doctrine it illustrates.

When I started in ministry, object lessons were in vogue. For the benefit of younger readers of this chapter, an object lesson is structured by using some simple object (watch, glasses, money, etc.) to teach (that's doctrine!) a lesson. Though not so much used these days (although some churches include a children's sermon in the morning service, which is essentially an object lesson, with or without an object), the Bible uses this method to teach some basic and important doctrines. Here are some of those illustrations with the doctrines they teach. The illustrations are not necessarily objects that could be brought to the desk or pulpit. In some cases it would be appropriate and useful to do so, but often well-chosen words will describe the biblical illustration.

EXAMPLES IN JEREMIAH

Jeremiah's command not to marry and have children (16:2). Marriage and family were cherished in Judaism, so for God to deny Jeremiah these blessings showed the extent and intensity of God's coming judgment on apostate Judah when normal relationships would be totally disrupted. Jeremiah's obedience attested to his total dedication to God's calling on his life. See 1 Corinthians 7:32–35 and Romans 12:1–2. The principal lesson: total dedication.

The potter (18:1–23). Explain how a potter used the wheel to make vessels and how he would simply make another vessel if the first one were somehow spoiled (v. 4). Actually one could show an inexpensive clay pot. This vividly illustrates the sovereignty of God, the Potter, over all nations, though not capriciously but with sensitivity to the possibility of their repenting (v. 8). Other Scriptures on this subject include Daniel 4:28–37 and Romans 9:20–24. The principal lesson: God is sovereign over all. Explain that *sovereignty* means "supremacy" and that God's sovereignty sometimes acts directly and often indirectly. Sovereignty does not mean God is a dictator, for he regularly involves our actions. Compare Acts 5:1–11 as an example of God's direct intervention and Romans 1:24, 26, 28 of his taking his hands off and letting people go their own wicked ways.

The broken jar (19:10). This illustration shows how God would smash Judah in the coming captivity. In this lesson an inexpensive clay pot could be thrown down and smashed in front of the audience. Depending on the time and number of messages available, you could use this to survey the history of the Jewish people after the captivity, including the return of some; their status under Roman rule at the time of Christ; their scattering among the nations today; the establishing of the political nation Israel; and their regathering, conversion and participation in the millennial kingdom (Rom. 11:25–29 among other Scriptures). The principal doctrine: Israelology.

Bonds and yokes on Jeremiah's neck (27:2). Ambassadors of the nations listed in verse 3 had gathered in Jerusalem to conspire with Judah to attempt to overthrow Nebuchadnezzar, king of Babylon. But Jeremiah warned the people that such a conspiracy would result in slavery (illustrated by the bonds and yokes) and that only by submitting to Nebuchadnezzar could they hope to survive. The principal lesson: submission to government. God who made the earth and all that is in it has the right to give the governing of it to whomever he wishes (v. 5) and for whatever length of time he wishes (v. 7). Use Daniel 4:17 also.

Jeremiah's purchasing a field in Anathoth (32:1–34). This action assured that Israel would one day be restored to its land. When this purchase took place, the Babylonians were besieging Jerusalem, having already captured Anathoth. To redeem a field that was then worthless showed Jeremiah's faith in God's greatness, majesty, and love (vv. 16–18). Here one could focus on Israel's future when God fulfills his promise of a new covenant (vv. 37–44 and 31:31–34). These five illustrations from Jeremiah could be used in a series on the history of Israel from Judah's captivity onward. The principal doctrine concerns the certainty of a future for Israel because of God's promises. Romans 11:29 would serve as a great New Testament text.

EXAMPLES IN THE TEACHINGS OF OUR LORD

People generally have some sense of how the Lord used illustrations in his teaching. Here are some of them, and in some cases the objects could be shown in the class or pulpit (e.g., salt, speck and plank, a child). Seeing the objects while being taught the lesson will help the listeners remember.

Salt and light (Matt. 5:13–16). Salt cleanses (Christ's followers should try to keep the world as clean as possible). Salt preserves (preserves good and slows corruption). Salt creates thirst (when others see what Christ's followers have, they may want some). Salt savors (gives a distinct and attractive taste, cf. Col. 4:6). Light gives direction and exposes darkness (Eph. 5:11–13).

Combine these images with a concordance study of salt and light for in-depth teaching that might evolve into a helpful series. The principal doctrine: the Christian's responsibility to the world in which he lives.

Birds and flowers (Matt. 6:26–34). God will take care of his children, sometimes miraculously but usually through natural means. Our priorities need to put his kingdom first, not things. These two teachings, trust and priorities, are summarized in verses 33–34.

Speck and plank (Matt. 7:3). This passage (vv. 1–5) teaches an often misunderstood concept of proper and improper judging of others. If one is in a spiritual condition (plank-free eyesight) in which you see clearly to judge and help remove specks from others, then this judging is not only proper but necessary as we relate to other believers. Note that planks and specks illustrate sins in ours and others' lives and show that while all sins are sin, some sins are worse or greater than others (cf. John 19:11). The principal doctrine: right and wrong judging of others.

Seven parables (Matt. 13). These illustrate various aspects of the present church age. The principal doctrine: ecclesiology, especially related to the characteristics of the present church period.

A little child (Matt. 18:1–6). Childlike characteristics of trust, openness, and eagerness to learn are necessary to enter the kingdom and to be great in it. Note also that our Lord taught that young children (the word *young* means "of young age") can believe (v. 6). The principal doctrine: soteriology.

The lost coin (Luke 15:8–9). The silver coin used here is a drachma, which was the price of a sheep. When using this illustration, substitute a twenty- or fifty-dollar bill because even finding a coin might not motivate someone to go to the trouble of retrieving it. The eagerness with which the woman searched for the coin shows God's great concern and love for lost sinners. Again this falls in the category of the doctrine of salvation.

The camel and the eye of a needle (Matt. 19:24). *Needle* means "a sewing needle" (not some small gate in a wall), which makes the comparison with a camel attempting to squeeze through it more vivid. Our Lord is not saying that wealthy people cannot be saved but that it is more difficult since such people seldom sense their personal need as readily as poorer folks do. It further emphasizes that only the miraculous and supernatural grace of God can do what is otherwise impossible. The principal doctrine: soteriology.

EXAMPLES FROM PAUL

The potter (Rom. 9:19–22). This passage with its illustration of the potter relates to the difficult doctrines of sovereignty and predestination. In particular, the potter illustration answers the question, if God does what he wants to do, then how can he blame people for what they do since they are only doing God's will (vv. 18–19)? Or to put it another way, if God has mercy on whom he desires and hardens whom he desires (v. 18), isn't that fatalism? Paul's reply is the potter illustration. If a potter can do what he wishes with the vessels he is crafting, then certainly God can do what he wishes with his vessels. We, in turn, must bow to his wisdom and trust him to do what will bring the most glory to him, even though we cannot understand. The principal doctrine: the sovereignty of God, which is a part of "theology proper" or the doctrine of God.

The olive tree (Rom. 11:17–28). Here Paul illustrates the rejection of Israel, his turning then to the Gentiles, and the ultimate restoration of Israel. The olive tree is the place of privilege before God, and its root is the Abrahamic covenant, which included blessings to both Jews and Gentiles. Israel, the natural branches, first occupied the place of privilege in God's plan. Then God set aside Israel because of their unbelief and grafted Gentiles into the place of privilege. But God will turn again to the Jewish people, and at the return of Christ all living Jews will turn to him and be saved. There are a number of doctrines here—the promises of the Abrahamic covenant (Gen. 12:1–3; 15:1–21), the choosing of Israel (Amos 3:2), their unbelief and his turning to the Gentiles (Acts 15:14), and their salvation at the return of Christ (Rom. 11:25). The teachings relate to Israelology and eschatology.

The bread and cup (1 Cor. 11:17–34). In this well-known passage, not only is the significance of the bread and cup paramount, but several other doctrines are included. For example, the love feast (vv. 17–23), the second coming of Christ (v. 26), the need for self-examination (vv. 27–29), and one reason for sickness and physical death (v. 30).

Husbands and wives (Eph. 5:22–23). This illustrates the relationship between Christ and his church. Don't let the illustration overwhelm the point so that the passage turns into a marriage manual. Though useful in that way, it primarily directs our focus on the believer's relationship to his or her Lord. From this perspective believers are to submit to the leadership of the Lord "in everything" (v. 24) and revere him (v. 33—the word *pheobomai*, "to stand in awe"). Further, Christ assuredly loves us, the epitome of which was his total, complete, once-for-all sacrifice on the cross (v. 25), and we must allow him to sanctify and mature us (vv. 26 and 29).

Ultimately he will present us holy and blameless (as Christ is, 1 Pet. 1:18). Doctrines taught include areas of Christology, soteriology, sanctification, and glorification.

Various illustrations of the believer (2 Tim. 2:1–6, 24–26).

- Soldier (vv. 3–4). He suffers hardship and is totally focused on pleasing his commander.
- Athlete (v. 5). He follows the rules (the Word of God).
- Farmer (v. 6). He receives a reward.
- Slave (vv. 24–26). He patiently seeks to bring remedial correction to wayward people.

All these fall into the category of sanctification.

EXAMPLES FROM PETER

1. Silver and gold contrasted to the blood of Christ (1 Pet. 1:18–19). The principal doctrine: Soteriology.
2. The fading nature of grass and flowers compared to the enduring character of the Word of God (1 Pet. 1:24–25). The principal doctrine: Bibliology.
3. As babies desire milk, so also should believers long for the Word of God in order to grow (1 Pet. 2:2). In this verse milk does not stand in contrast to solid food (as it does in 1 Cor. 3:2 and Heb. 5:12) but includes all of the Word. The principal doctrine: sanctification.
4. Follow in his steps (1 Pet. 2:21). Christ serves as the example that we believers are to follow. The well-known book *In His Steps* by Charles Sheldon is based on this verse, as well as the WWJD (What Would Jesus Do?) emphasis.

5. Clothe yourself with humility; wrap humility around
    yourself (1 Pet. 5:5). Here a clear and exact definition
    of *humility* is necessary. Also contrast it with pride. A
    concordance study of these two words will flesh out
    this teaching.

6. Satan is likened to a lion (1 Pet. 5:8–9). Describe a
    lion making a kill as illustrative of Satan's attacks on
    believers. In Hebrews 11:29 the word *devour* is trans-
    lated "drowned" to describe the destruction of the
    Egyptians as they pursued the Israelites fleeing from
    Egypt. Likewise Satan wants to destroy completely the
    testimony of believers. Don't overlook the defenses we
    have against Satan's attacks (be sober and on the
    alert). The principal doctrine: Satan.

7. Unfruitful (2 Pet. 1:8). Even believers can become
    unfruitful and useless or barren although every
    Christian will bear some fruit during his Christian life
    (1 Cor. 4:5).

Studious and even casual reading of the Scriptures will
bring to mind other biblical illustrations on which doctrines
are built. And just because illustrations are basic and uncom-
plicated, the doctrines may be more easily memorable.

EXAMPLES ESPECIALLY FOR CHILDREN

When using various kinds of illustrations to communicate
doctrine to children, keep in mind these suggestions (which
can also be relevant in teaching adults!).

First, use everyday illustrations and objects, things that can be found around the house. Using illustrations familiar to children serves two purposes: the child will already be familiar with the object and will not have to have it explained, and the child will see the object in daily activities and be reminded of the lesson it illustrates.

Second, substitute simple labels that are less theological than the ones we tend to use. For example, instead of "eternal security," use "safe forever." Instead of "casual Christian," use "self-centered Christian." Rather than "rapture" try "the big snatch." Instead of "the tribulation" substitute "time of big trouble." Rather than "advocate" use "somebody who takes your side." One important caveat: "dumbing down" is inappropriate with many audiences who need rather to be stretched to understand and use theological terms. That cliché, "Put the cookies on the lower shelf," is appropriate for small people whose reach is limited physically, intellectually, and/or spiritually. But if you do not make people stretch and expand their understanding, you will end up with stooped, hunchbacked Christians who can't stand up tall.

Here are some examples appropriate to help children understand doctrine.

"Underneath are the everlasting arms" (Deut. 33:27). Show God's care for us by lifting up a child, using your arms underneath his or her body. Explain how safe this makes us forever, for God's arms never get tired and never need rest.

"But the very hairs of your head are all numbered" (Matt. 10:30). God knows everything about us and also about everything. The number of hairs varies on all our heads. God knows the exact count. Pull one out, and he knows how many are left. There are roughly 103,000 black hairs on a head, 110,000 brown ones, and 140,000 blond ones.

A false or fake savior can seem to be the same as Christ, the true and only Savior; but the fake will only lead followers to hell. Use a packet of sugar substitute (like Equal or Sweet'nLow). The fake sweeteners may look and taste like real sugar, but you usually cannot bake with them because they become bitter when heated. Fake saviors, no matter how attractive they may seem to be, cannot withstand the fire of hell. Trust the only true Savior, our Lord Jesus.

Any book on object lessons will generate additional ideas.[1]

Finally, don't accept the premise that children are too young to understand doctrinal truths. Sometimes teachers are too complicated, but a child's mind is receptive and malleable, and you are an important force in helping mold it.

Chapter Seven

———◆———

OF THE MAKING
OF PRINCIPLES THERE SEEMS
TO BE NO END

THE CONCEPT

By seeking to use (and sometimes to misuse) principles, I mean extracting from the biblical text principles and then applying them to the contemporary audience or situation. Although not necessarily an improper sequence, in practice the reverse often happens. That is, we look at the audience, then search for a principle we want to promote to that audience and then try to find a passage to support it. Underlying the reverse procedure lies the assumption that we know what the people need to hear. Of course, that is often true; a leader who knows a group from contacts other than when he is preaching or teaching will be able to discern some needs. Too, there exist in every generation and almost every group some basic needs that the Bible addresses and for which extracting principles will not involve an artificial or forced use of the biblical text.

SOME DANGERS

We must not think that studying and preaching doctrines exempt one from the misuse of principles just because the material is doctrinal. Indeed, if doctrine is important, then the danger of abusing principles in relation to doctrine is even more significant. It is tempting to minimize a doctrine from which principles are extracted and emphasize only the principles. To do this may result in failure to communicate the underlying doctrinal truths.

SOME EXAMPLES

All the examples in this section I have personally heard or read or been connected with in some way, and all came from evangelicals.

A danger exists in attempting to make the facts in a text teach something that is in reality not in the text. For instance, I heard a sermon on Genesis 14:22, just the part containing the name of God as the Most High and possessor of heaven and earth. The principle drawn from this phrase was that since God is the Sovereign Creator of heaven and earth, this lays upon us a mandate to evangelize the world. Of course, evangelizing is commanded of believers but not from this text by any stretch of exegetical imagination or machination. Obviously the speaker wanted to emphasize the duty to witness, and he said he wanted to show this was commanded throughout the entire Bible, so he had to find a text (actually a pretext) in Genesis. In his zeal to make a point about witnessing (which is important), he almost completely neglected expounding from that text an important aspect of the doctrine of God, and he totally ignored the context which shows Abraham's humility and faith.

On another occasion a preacher who practices healings found his principle for doing so in Galatians 5:22 in the word *chrestotes*, which means "goodness, kindness, generosity, uprightness." He did give those meanings (or some of them) and then added "with a healing touch" as if that phrase was part of the meaning and therefore part of the text. Thus he concluded that the fruit of the Spirit, which includes goodness, means goodness with a healing touch. If one believes in supernatural healings today, other and better verses can certainly be found. Again he was so intent on trying to find a biblical basis for healing from the verse that he completely ignored one of the clear aspects of the fruit of the Spirit.

It is dangerous to approach the study and exegesis of a text with the goal of finding analogies between the original audience to whom the text was addressed and the contemporary one the speaker is addressing. Sometimes such an approach will stretch the text beyond its intent, selectively use parts of the text that "fit," or completely misuse the text.

To put it bluntly, this approach can be stated as "looking for something that will preach!"

An example: the title of the message was "How Much Does God Love the World?" The speaker used two texts. The first was Jonah 3–4 to show how much God loved the world in Old Testament times. But he never explained that the evangelism of the Ninevites was an exception; the usual way a Gentile could become right with God under the Mosaic Law involved becoming a proselyte to Judaism. He never mentioned that God on occasion commanded the destruction, not the evangelization, of Israel's Gentile enemies. That would have spoiled his selectively extracted principle from Jonah.

His second text (in the same message) was John 3:16. In expounding this text, his points were that God loved the world so much that (1) he sent the Son, (2) sacrificed the Son, and (3) separated himself from the Son on the cross. Then the principles he derived were that (1) we are sent into the world, (2) we should live sacrificially, but he was forced to omit the third principle because believers will never be separated from God. The text declares what God did in sending his Son and our responsibility to believe. It says nothing about our being sent or sacrificial living. An important Christological and soteriological text was stripped of its doctrine.

To extract principles that are not there often necessarily requires spiritualizing or deliteralizing the biblical text. A guest preacher on a well-respected and long-standing radio program spoke at length of acacia or shittim wood, which he said was a picture of the brokenness God wants believers to be. The principle of brokenness is biblical but has nothing to do with acacia wood, even as an illustration. He said the wood was twisted and fit only for burning. Likewise God disciplines us so we can be broken. Then when we are broken, God will cover us with gold just as he commanded the acacia wood to be so covered in the tabernacle. His conclusion: brokenness is the way to shine for Christ.

I searched Bible dictionaries to educate myself about acacia wood. Nowhere could I find that it was twisted, though it did make good charcoal. It had a thick trunk and a spreading crown ten to eighteen feet tall. Furthermore, I searched to see when acacia wood was covered with gold and found that the ark, staves, table of bread, and pillars were but that the boards were not, and the altar was covered with bronze. So how could I be assured that if I was broken I would be covered with gold? I might end up being covered with bronze or simply be a wooden board! Of all the sermons I have heard and read, this one comes close to being the epitome of twisting (pun intended!), selectively using, and deliteralizing the meaning of the biblical text.

Another example was extracted from 2 Chronicles 12:9–10. When Shishak looted the temple of the golden shields Solomon had made, Rehoboam replaced them with shields of bronze. The principle: we should never settle for less than the best.

In another instance, Matthew 9:17, about putting new wine in old wineskins, was said to teach a principle that validates changes in the order or style of worship services.

At least three ramifications result by this kind of mishandling of the text. First, it demeans the text itself. Second, it gives the impression that the principle has the same authority as the biblical text; and, third, it makes the hearer think that since he could never find such wonderful insights from the text, studying the Bible on his own is not much use. The response to such messages is often, "Wasn't that wonderful? I never saw that in that passage." The truth is that it wasn't wonderful, and you didn't see it simply because it wasn't there in the text.

Unsubstantiated principles can offer false promises when used without the restraints in the text itself. One evangelical pastor/evangelist said on TV that if God can find ten righteous people in a neighborhood today he will spare that neighborhood from hoodlums and various crimes. Then he went on to suggest this principle could be expanded to more neighborhoods and then to a city, etc. This "promise" on which he based this principle was Abraham's pleading with God in Genesis 18:32 where God said he would spare Sodom and Gomorrah if he could find ten righteous people in these cities. To find ten righteous people in any neighborhood is a worthy goal, but to attach a promise that guarantees sparing neighborhoods totally lacks biblical support. Indeed, there must be hundreds of examples where God did not spare areas wherein there were more than ten righteous people.

Another favorite promise passage used over and over is 2 Chronicles 7:14. The clear context of the promise relates to the dedication of Solomon's temple in Jerusalem. After Solomon's magnificent prayer and the offering of the multitude of sacrifices, God appeared to Solomon at night and reiterated the necessity of walking with God and punishment if he did not do so. While one may use verse 14 as a general principle of the requirements for blessing being humility, prayer, devotion, and repentance, the specific blessing promised in this verse is the healing of the land of Israel when "My people"—that is, Israel—repents. To stretch this promise to assure blessing on any nation whose citizens repent is simply that—a stretch, though admittedly an appealing one. Too often this verse serves as a call to God's people (Christians) to repent in order to heal (that is, preserve) our land (America). As far as I can discern, there is no promise in the Bible that America will be preserved even if the population were 100 percent believers. To be sure, this verse contains an important principle: repentance on the part of God's people brings individual blessing, but it does not contain a promise that the blessing will extend to the nation of those people. An individual and specific promise has undergone a metamorphosis into a general principle supposedly applicable to many other nations. It would be better to use Proverbs 14:34: "Righteousness exalts a nation, but sin is a disgrace to any people."

SOME GUIDELINES

Always ask if there is a solid exegetical base in the text for the principle. If not, do not yield to the temptation to invent one or to proceed on a shaky base. While there are analogies between physical and spiritual blindness in John 9, the text does not introduce the subject of spiritual blindness until verse 39. The first part of the chapter teaches important truths about the doctrine of sickness (which is certainly relevant). It is always best and safest to stick to the text.

A message I heard on the good Samaritan (Luke 10:29–37) had these three alliterated points: the hurting world, the hesitant church, and the healing stranger. Exegetically, the purpose of the parable was to answer the lawyer's question, Who is my neighbor? This was not addressed in the message.

Guard any legitimate principle not only by the text from which it comes but the context, immediate and wider. Sometimes we try to encourage someone who is going through a difficult time by quoting Genesis 50:20: "You meant evil against me, but God meant it for good." That may be applicable in some cases, but we must also remember the many instances cited in Hebrews 11:36–37 that had different, even opposite, outcomes in the will of God.

Be careful about taking commands or illustrations from the way God has worked in the past and using them as commands or illustrations for this time. For example, the food prohibitions in the Mosaic Law (Deut. 14:1–21) have been thankfully superceded by the permission of 1 Timothy 4:3. Yet in my lifetime books advocating the Mosaic guidelines about food have appeared promising good health if they are followed.

One homiletical paradigm goes like this.

> Exegesis (the basis in the ancient biblical text)
> Timeless theological principles (the bridge)
> Preaching application (to the contemporary time and audience)

But the weaknesses in the paradigm are the unanswered questions that relate to those "timeless theological principles."

Are you sure the principles come from the exegesis? Are they really timeless? How can one be sure these are correct principles?

If I have seemed to come on too strong in this chapter, it is only because I feel that too much Bible study and preaching, while not necessarily unbiblical, is based on weak, shaky, selective, or deliteralized handling of biblical texts. Such mishandling or shallow handling of the Word of our Lord dishonors both the Word and the Lord.

Appendix One

◆

Expository Preaching Versus Not Unbiblical Preaching

Why state the title this way? Simply to try to present a sharp contrast between messages that are not unbiblical yet not expository from those that are expository. Of course, expository messages must be biblical. But many messages, though not unbiblical (positively stated that means they relate to the Bible), are not expository. An expository sermon has to be biblical. But a biblical (which means the same as "not unbiblical") message does not guarantee its being expository.

Add to this mix, the type of message commonly called "topical" often leads to more confusion. Can a topical message be expository? Yes. Will it necessarily be so? No. A topical message can also be not unbiblical without being expository.

The image some preachers have of exposition is taking a section of Scripture and analyzing and explaining it almost word for word. Because topical preaching almost always involves several passages of Scripture, some assume that it cannot be expository simply because it doesn't stick to one passage. Too, not unbiblical preaching may involve more than one passage, even though one passage may serve as the starting point for the sermon. Yet the passages may not be treated in an expository way. Topical exposition will stick to the topic and explain the passages involved in an expository manner. Not unbiblical topical messages often loosely use other passages, which are only more or less remotely related to the topic. Words, sentiments, ideas from several passages may have a commonality, but that does not assure that the passages are truly expounded.

Look at this example of a nonexpository but not unbiblical message (published in an evangelical institution's publicity piece).

The title of the article/sermon was "God's Plan for Success." (In the development of this subject, the success concerned that of a church, not an individual.) The biblical text (printed out separately) was Acts 4:31–33. The outline included five points that were not unbiblical, but neither were they used in the article the way Luke used them in the text. The five ingredients for success were:

1. Great Praying (v. 31)
2. Great Power (v. 31)
3. Great Preaching (v. 31)
4. Great Partnership (v. 32)
5. Great Prosperity (v. 33)

Allow me a few observations. First, some key words were not carefully used. In verse 31 no distinction is made between the filling of the Spirit when *piplēmi* is used rather than *pleroō*. Boldness is only described as daring to say, "Thus says the Lord." Second, there is a selectivity in the use of verse 32. Partnership as unity within the church is the only part of that verse mentioned in the article; having possessions in common is entirely passed over. But in the text the "partnership" includes a union that was both spiritual and material. Why omit the material part? Because it did not fit the slant of the article. Selectivity also shows up in verse 33 where the content of the apostles' message, the resurrection, is not mentioned at all. Only prosperity is focused on in the article, and that idea is based on the use of the word *grace* in the text, a considerable stretch to have alliteration!

An expository dealing with these three verses would not permit selectivity or imprecise use of words. Not unbiblical preaching does, and though not necessarily wrong, it is different, insufficient, and gives a spin to the text that suits the author.

Another sermon I heard by a well-known evangelical titled "The Beginning of the Gospel" (Mark 1:1) was developed this way.

1. The Beginning in Heaven in the Counsels of God
2. The Beginning on Earth in the Prophets
3. The Beginning in Our Hearts

I am at a loss to know what category of messages this belongs to. Everything said was biblical. Was it topical? That would be a stretch. Was it expository? Certainly not.

WHAT IS EXPOSITORY PREACHING/TEACHING?

Most sermons preached by evangelicals are not unbiblical, but neither are they truly expository. Regrettably, some in the pulpit and in the pew do not know or recognize the difference. But there is a significant difference with important ramifications for communicating the truth of God's Word.

Of course, certain occasions expect messages or addresses or talks, which are not necessarily even biblical. But let the preacher/teacher/speaker be warned not to think that he and his audience are hearing something biblical. A Bible verse at the beginning used like a diving board to take off from or one at the end like a life preserver to rescue the talk does not transfigure or elevate or make authoritative the content in between.

First, we must (surprise!) define terms. *Expound, expose, exposition, expository* come from the Latin and mean "to explain or set forth." The dictionary defines it more fully as "a setting forth of the meaning or purpose [as of a writing] . . . designed to convey information or explain what is difficult to understand." *Preaching* also comes from the Latin and basically means "to make known in public." The dictionary states that meaning and adds ideas like "to urge acceptance or abandonment of an idea or course of action" and "to advocate earnestly."

Biblical terms for preaching include "to cheer with good tidings," "to declare," "to address a public assembly" (in the Old Testament), and "to announce," "to discourse," "to speak," "to herald," "to speak boldly."

Several other words are relevant to the concept of exposition. One is *diermeneuō*, which means "to translate" (as in Acts 9:36) or "explain/interpret" (as in verses relating to the gift of interpreting tongues [1 Cor. 12:30; 14:5]). The word occurs in Luke 24:27 to describe our Lord's explanation of Old Testament prophecies to the two disciples on the road to Emmaus. When expounding a passage, the preacher/teacher should translate the meaning of the text into explanatory language that conveys the meaning of the original and to do so to effect a change in the hearer.

Though the text does not use the word *expository*, Stephen's exposition of Old Testament history recorded in Acts 7:1–53 explains, supports, and hammers home his text: "You are doing just as your fathers did" (7:51—interesting that the text is at the end of the message). Further, he advocates earnestly for a change of heart in his hearers.

Second Timothy 2:15 instructs those who handle the word of truth to do it "accurately." The word means "to cut a path so that the traveler may go directly to his destination." It is also used of a mason cutting stones straight so as to fit into their proper places. Thus we should handle the Scripture in a straight manner, that is, correctly, soundly, and to the point.

Putting these ideas together, we can define exposition as follows. Expository preaching/teaching translates for the hearer the meaning of the text accurately so that the hearer can understand and then hopefully obey what God says.

Not unbiblical preaching/teaching means that although the content of the message is not contrary to the teachings of the Bible, it does not specifically expose what the text itself says. It usually does include the element of exhortation. Sadly, sometimes not unbiblical teaching majors on the hortatory and minors on the expository.

WHAT TOOLS ARE NECESSARY FOR EXPOSITORY PREACHING/TEACHING?

Neither the same tools nor every tool will necessarily be involved in preparing to expound a passage. But here are some basic ones.

The Historical Setting. Exposing the text necessitates clarifying all facets of its historical setting and background. For example, consider the various taxes imposed in New Testament times. There was the census tax which required payment with a specific coin and which went directly to Caesar (Matt. 22:15–22). Knowing these facts is essential to understanding our Lord's "render to Caesar . . . render to God." Additionally there was the two-dracma tax which was collected annually to support and refurbish the temple in Jerusalem (Matt. 17:24–27). How one became a tax collector of duties or customs on goods passing in and out of the country, of which Matthew was one, explains why the Pharisees condemned our Lord for eating with those tax collectors (Matt. 9:9–13). Other taxes to which people were subject in Old and New Testament times are described in Bible encyclopedias.

The Context of a Passage. Passages of Scripture ordinarily do not exist in isolation but in context. Not unbiblical preaching often tends to isolate verses from their context with the result that the interpretation is skewed toward the point the preacher wants to make. This may not be the point of the verse when the verse is considered in its context.

A message I heard took the point of view that Jacob was bargaining with God according to Genesis 28:20–22 and that neither he nor we can bargain with God. But more likely, according to the context (especially v. 15), Jacob was worshipfully vowing to acknowledge and believe the promise God had already made that Jacob would return to the land, and this promise was unrelated to any bargain or vow Jacob would make.

Again, more than once 1 Corinthians 2:9 is explained as indicating blessings believers will enjoy in the future in heaven. The verse sometimes is used at a funeral as a promise of what the deceased believer experiences in heaven after death. But verse 10 says in clear terms that the Holy Spirit has revealed these blessings here and now to the believer in this life.

For his Easter message a well-known evangelical chose Ephesians 2:1–9 (why not verse 10, which is the end of the section?). His major points were: (1) mankind is in a pit (his word for the substance of vv. 1–3); (2) mortality is mankind's greatest problem; and (3) Christ's resurrection gives us hope (v. 5, "made . . . alive"). But "made . . . alive" is not referring to future bodily resurrection, which is the cure for mortality, but to spiritual life which we possess now as believers. Too, mortality is actually a result of sin, which is man's greatest problem.

The Exegesis of a Passage. Careful exegesis is important in expository preaching. Without it there is no sure basis for declaring that this is what God is saying in that passage. Sometimes, when there seems to be more than one legitimate interpretation of a passage, one's theology may be the deciding factor as to which is the preferred meaning. Sometimes two possibilities may both be correct and should be combined in understanding the passage. Why must we decide whether "love of Christ" in 2 Corinthians 5:14 is a subjective genitive (my love for Christ) or an objective genitive (Christ's love for me)? Why not include both ideas that constrain me to witness?

Does Romans 1:4 ("resurrection from the dead") refer to Christ's own resurrection and/or the resurrections of those he raised during his earthly ministry? One may give preference to either view, or one may combine both views as evidences of the Lord's being proved to be the Son of God.

What tools can be used to accomplish solid exegesis? All can use an English dictionary, a concordance for the meaning of Greek and Hebrew words, a Bible dictionary, various translations, and commentaries based on the English text. Some of the greatest expositors did not know Greek and Hebrew. But if one does, then a new class of helps opens up, especially commentaries on the original Greek and Hebrew texts.

However, even commentaries fall into different categories. There are those written for the English reader only, even though the author of the commentary knows the original languages. There are those which offer detailed exegetical works on the original texts. Others might be classified as expositional surveys, and still others as mainly devotional (or homiletical). Some, of course, overlap several categories. But the plethora of helps available today is almost overwhelming in both amount and variety.

Most of us need help in choosing which books will be best for our needs and stage of intellectual and spiritual maturity. If one is building a library, especially on limited funds, my advice is to buy timeless books (including reference material) and borrow timely books that, though significant for a time, will not be particularly useful after a few years.

Zero in on Theme(s). Sometimes only one will be the focus of a message. Sometimes the passage will include several themes that may have to be treated separately or may be subsumed under one overarching theme. For example, in Philippians 2:17–30 Paul praises the Philippians for their sacrificial service to him (vv. 17–18) and commends Timothy for his selflessness (vv. 19–24) and Epaphroditus for his ministry to Paul and the Philippians (vv. 25–30). Each one of these could be a separate sermon, or they could be put together into one. I heard that done once under the title "Eulogies for the Living."

No message should be antibiblical. No message should be unbiblical. Hopefully all Bible messages should be not only biblical but also expository. This requires the messenger to be a careful and skilled craftsman to express accurately the meaning of God's Word and in so doing to honor it and him. What the Bible says is the most important part of any message, so let it speak accurately, clearly, and powerfully.

A side note: If a service or situation includes the public reading of the Scripture, please do not limit that reading to a few verses. What God says in the Bible is far more important than any other part of a service and should be paramount. To help achieve this goal, a friend of mine recently began the practice of reading the entire passage(s) he would preach from before his exposition and then also at the conclusion of the message. That's a great way to help implant the message on the minds and hearts of the hearers.

Consider also the restrictions that projecting the Scripture onto a screen place on the audience. It makes carrying one's Bible unnecessary. It limits looking at the wider context. It makes it impossible for the hearer to look up other passages that may come to mind as the sermon or lesson progresses. Projecting a Scripture passage may have its usefulness, but it should never downplay or replace having a Bible in hand and open. If visuals are used, let them be as a supplement, not a substitute. One positive use of showing Scripture on a screen is to use the screen for reading the Scripture aloud in unison. If the audience has the same translation available (in the pews or chairs, for example), then it would be preferable, in my opinion, to read together from open Bibles. But since so many different translations are used today, it is becoming more difficult to have everybody read together unless Bibles are furnished. Reading from the screen would be an effective way to have all participate. But again, a group looking at a screen should never replace the ideal of individuals looking at their own open Bibles.

A WORD ABOUT ALLITERATION

We who speak certainly want our audience to remember at least something about what we say. In some circles and with many speakers, alliteration has become the standard of a good message and the guarantee of remembering it. Neither is necessarily true.

Of course, if alliteration helps people to remember, use it. However, too often words that alliterate are forced onto the text rather than arising out of it. Preaching or teaching through an interpreter in a language that is not his native tongue will quickly show the uselessness, if not impossibility, of alliteration. Years ago I had the opportunity to preach regularly at church services exclusively for boys and girls ages nine through twelve. A few adults were also present to serve as monitors. The format of the services was "church," not Sunday school, not child evangelism. My part was the sermon. I resisted the easier path of storytelling and decided to teach/preach Romans. Further, I encouraged the kids to bring Bibles and pencils because the Lord put in my mind building the messages on specific words in the biblical text. These highlighted words, which I asked the kids to underline or bracket in their own Bibles, served as the points of the message. Of course they could rarely be alliterated, but they were remembered. Often parents would tell me what I had preached to their children, and they got that information from their children and not from being present in the service. That experience taught me a great method.

SOME THOUGHTS ABOUT APPLICATION

Exposition by definition includes the facet of change because of what has been explained. Thus application and persuasion are expected aspects of an expository message.

Nevertheless, application involves a number of related things: the biblical text (the basis for what to change), spiritual state of the hearer (the individual's need for change), relevance (the appropriateness of the particular change), presentation of the speaker (*an*, not *the*, agent of change), the human will (the center for change), and the Holy Spirit (the necessary power for change). Let's examine these elements.

Since the Word of God is basic to all the elements in change, then it must be given prominence and careful exposition in a consistent, methodical, whole-counsel-of-God way. Picking and choosing from here and there what I think people need will not produce a well-rounded Christian. To be sure, there are occasions when one will depart from a planned series to insert a special theme.

In attempting to apply any exposition, there will be varying responses simply because in every audience varying states of physical, emotional, and spiritual growth will be present. Even in an audience of one, there will be multiple needs. Some in an audience may be unsaved; others, carnal believers; others who need encouragement, not conviction; and still others, who have dozed through the entire message! The Holy Spirit knows all the needs in each hearer, and we must trust him to use something said to meet a need.

What of relevance? Let's be clear about one main thing. God's Word does not have to be made relevant. It is so. All of us have to be made relevant to it as the supreme standard. To say we must make its teachings relevant to a twenty-first-century society, or a post-Christian world, or to specialized groups is to say God's revelation is insufficient. The Bible was written in a pre-Christian world that was characterized by all the needs and sins of the twenty-first-century. However, for people to acknowledge relevance may take time, many exposures to the Word, and little steps of response.

Applications will often be obvious, but sometimes they will be subtle and not easily discovered. If that be the case, then resist the temptation to force or drag from the text something not there. Better to let the Holy Spirit apply the passage, which he may do in ways I could never have conceived.

Once in discussing Isaiah 2:1–5, which was an assignment for student preaching, I asked the professor why he included verse 5. It seemed to me to begin a new direction in the text. Verses 1–4 speak in detail about the future millennial kingdom. In verse 5 Isaiah turns to the then present need for Israel to purge herself of many sins. The professor acknowledged that verse 5 was in reality a new turn in the text but that he wanted it a part of the sermon so that verses 1–4 could be applied by using verse 5 since there was not an obvious application in verses 1–4!

Rigid homiletical guidelines usually place the application at the last part of the message. First, one exegetes the text; second, one finds a theological or subject bridge that brings the text into the present; and finally, one applies the text to the audience. This may be a helpful general guideline, but one should not be afraid of changing it. Notice the structure of Philippians 2. The exhortation to apply what Paul will write in the following verses is first (vv. 1–4); then follows the doctrine on which it is based (the kenosis of Christ, vv. 5–11), then further application to the Philippians' circumstances (vv. 12–18), concluding with illustrations from the lives of Timothy and Epaphroditus (vv. 19–30).

Structure, firm; pattern, flexible.

Application, exhortation, and relevance have their proper functions. Yet I must remember that while I can try to influence the choices of the human will, I cannot force a person to make the right choices. Even salvation, the gift of God (Eph. 2:9), involves the individual's faith (Rom. 4:5).

The written Word of God must be primary. The spoken exposition of that Word must be accurate and persuasive. The Word heard will hopefully result in obedience.

"For the word of God is living and active and sharper than any two-edged sword, and piercing as far as the division of soul and spirit, of both joints and marrow, and able to judge the thoughts and intentions of the heart" (Heb. 4:12).

"All Scripture is inspired by God and profitable for teaching, for reproof, for correction, for training in righteousness; so that the man of God may be adequate, equipped for every good work" (2 Tim. 3:16–17).

Therefore—"preach the word" (2 Tim. 4:2).

Appendix Two

───────◆───────

Outline Versus List

The Difference between an Outline and a List

What's the difference between an outline and a list? A list is similar to the materials you gather in order to build something. An outline is similar to the structure or design you give to those materials that results in the finished product.

Having the proper tools is obviously part of the process. If you were to decide to build a bookcase, you would likely make a list of materials needed before going to the hardware store to buy them. Then, using your tools, you would build the bookcase according to a design you have outlined either in your mind or sketched on paper. Clearly you usually need a list, tools, and an outline—the structure.

In preparing a sermon or lesson, you need to jot down all the ideas and notes that come to mind as you study the passage, then use the tools (concordance, dictionary, commentaries) to be certain you understand your notes correctly, then structure them with an outline for presentation. Here is a different example.

The subject: A Dinner Party

A List for the Party	An Outline of the Party
1. Iron the tablecloths.	I. The Preparations for the Party
2. Buy place cards.	(# 1, 2, 5, 9)
3. Decide on appetizers.	II. The Menu for the Party
4. Get out dominoes sets.	(# 3, 7, 8)
5. Set up card tables.	III. The Entertainment at the
	Party (# 4, 6)

6. Arrange travel pictures.

7. Marinate meat.

8. Decide on dessert.

9. Purchase salad ingredients.

SOME CAVEATS IN OUTLINING

Subpoints must always relate to the point under which they are put. Roman numerals (I, II, III), must explain the main title of the message. Letters (A, B, C) cannot jump over the Roman numerals to refer back to the title. In the illustration above about a dinner party, dominoes cannot refer directly back to the title. It must be under its "boss" heading which was "Entertainment." Whatever scheme of numbering you use, this relationship of subpoints to the boss points must not be violated. Thus:

TITLE

I.

    A.

        1.

        2.

    B.

II.

Not to do this will blur and confuse the relationship and even the importance of the points in the outline.

In the same type of headings (e.g., Roman numerals, capital letters, arabic numbers, etc.), do not mix verbs, nouns, adjectives, etc. If the Roman numeral headings use a single word, all of those headings must use a single word and the same part of speech. If a phrase, then all must be phrases with the same part of speech outstanding. The same goes for the subpoints. However, in my opinion, the 1s, 2s, 3s can be, for example, single words under A and phrases under B.

Do not think that a passage is subject to only one outline as long as each outline comes from the text. For example, here are several bare (not filled in) outlines that could be found in 1 Thessalonians 1.

Title: How Can You Know You Are Elect? (v. 4)
  I. The Word came to you (v. 5).
  II. The Word sounded out from you (v. 8).
  III. The unbelievers said so (vv. 9–10).

Title: What Characterizes a Healthy Church?
  I. It consists of saved people (v. 5).
  II. It has maturing people (v. 6).
  III. It has missionary-minded people (v. 8).
  IV. It has serving people (v. 9).

Title: A Great Testimony (vv. 9–10) *or* A Report Card
  I. The Origin of the Report—Unbelievers
  II. The Subject of the Report—Paul's Ministry
  III. The Content of the Report: Saved, Serving, Waiting

Avoid assuming that alliteration is necessary or even desirable. Any alliteration must come naturally, rather than being forced, and should use words that people understand. Use a dictionary if you wish to help find an alliterative word, but be sparing in the use of a thesaurus. Remember that even similar words usually need more precise defining; e.g., think, cogitate, reflect, reason, speculate, deliberate, ponder. Always be precise in the words you choose to use.

Let's go back to the original illustration about building a bookcase. Remember that the primary purpose of a bookcase, however decorative it might be, is to hold the books so they can be easily used. Therefore, though outlining is important for analyzing, prioritizing, and formalizing material, it is that material, the Word of God, that is of the utmost importance. Indeed, I think that some sermons might be more effective by simply reading the Bible aloud rather than using a poor outline that may confuse or bore, or a dazzling outline that takes center stage away from the biblical text.

Not only is good outlining important for the presentation to the hearers, but it is also necessary for the presenter. It not only gives structure to the material, but it also brings to the fore matters of priority and relationships within the material. This should keep the items pointed in the right direction, related properly to one another, and put together in a way that keeps the focus of the text clear.

NOTES

Chapter 1, Is Doctrine Really That Important?

1. J. C. Ryle, *Christian Leaders of the Eighteenth Century* (Carlisle, Penn.: Banner of Truth, 1978), 430.

2. David Wells, "Seminaries and the Death of Theology," *The Dallas/Fort Worth Heritage*, January 1999, 34, 49.

3. "By common confession, great is the mystery of godliness:
   He who was revealed in the flesh,
   Was vindicated in the Spirit,
   Seen by angels,
   Proclaimed among the nations,
   Believed on in the world,
   Taken up in glory." (1 Tim. 3:16)

4. "But solid food is for the mature, who because of practice have their senses trained to discern good and evil" (Heb. 5:14).

5. "Teaching them to observe all that I commanded you." Notice the same twofold emphasis: "teaching" (doctrine) and "observe" (practice).

Chapter 2, Communicating Doctrine by Using Major Bible Passages

1. *The Dallas Morning News*, 23 June 2002, 19A.

2. Significant Old Testament passages include Leviticus 27:30–33; Deuteronomy 14:22–27; Malachi 3:8.

3. "So that He would be just and the justifier of the one who has faith in Jesus" (Rom. 3:26b).

4. A list of central or major passages for the usual categories of systematic theology can be found in my book, *Basic Theology* (Chicago: Moody Press, 1999), 613–19.

Chapter 3, Communicating Doctrine by Using Systematic Theology

1. Charles Haddon Spurgeon, *Lectures to My Students* (Grand Rapids: Zondervan, 1945), 196.

Chapter 4, Communicating Doctrine from the Perspective of Biblical Theology

1. Jews denied canonical status to the Old Testament Apocrypha, and it was never included in the Hebrew canon. Manuscripts of the Septuagint (a Greek translation of the Old Testament made in the third century BC) include the Apocrypha as an addendum to the Old Testament as did Latin Bibles, which were translated from the Greek.

Chapter 5, Teaching Doctrine from a Concordance

1. I wrote in more detail on this subject in *Balancing the Christian Life* (Chicago: Moody, 1969), chapter 10.

Chapter 6, Teaching Doctrine from Biblical Illustrations

1. The one I wrote is *Object Lessons* (Chicago: Moody, 1981). There are one hundred ideas in this book.